The Art of Living

EPICTETUS

GENERAL PRESS

Published by
GENERAL PRESS
4805/24, Fourth Floor, Krishna House
Ansari Road, Daryaganj, New Delhi - 110002
Ph : 011-23282971, 45795759
E-mail : generalpressindia@gmail.com

www.generalpress.in

First Edition : 2022

ISBN : 9789354993817

Published by Azeem Ahmad Khan for General Press

Contents

1

Some things are in our control and others not. Things in our control are opinion, pursuit, desire, aversion, and, in a word, whatever are our own actions. Things not in our control are body, property, reputation, command, and, in one word, whatever are not our own actions.

The things in our control are by nature free, unrestrained, unhindered; but those not in our control are weak, slavish, restrained, belonging to others. Remember, then, that if you suppose that things which are slavish by nature are also free, and that what belongs to others is your own, then you will be hindered. You will lament, you will be disturbed, and you will find fault both with gods and men. But if you suppose that only to be your own which is your own, and what belongs to others such as it really is, then no one will ever compel you or restrain you. Further, you will find fault with no one or accuse no one. You will do nothing against your will. No one will hurt you, you will have no enemies, and you not be harmed.

Aiming therefore at such great things, remember that you must not allow yourself to be carried, even with a slight tendency, towards the attainment of lesser things. Instead, you must entirely quit some things and for the present postpone the rest. But if you would both have these great things, along with power and riches, then you will not gain even the latter, because you aim at the former too: but you will absolutely fail of the former, by which alone happiness and freedom are achieved.

Work, therefore to be able to say to every harsh appearance, "You are but an appearance, and not absolutely the thing you appear to be." And then examine it by those rules which you have, and first, and chiefly, by this: whether it concerns the things which are in our own control, or those which are not; and, if it concerns anything not in our control, be prepared to say that it is nothing to you.

2

Remember that following desire promises the attainment of that of which you are desirous; and aversion promises the avoiding that to which you are averse. However, he who fails to obtain the object of his desire is disappointed, and he who incurs the object of his aversion wretched. If, then, you confine your aversion to those objects only which are contrary to the natural use of your faculties, which you have in your own control, you will never incur anything to which you are averse. But if you are averse to sickness, or death, or poverty, you will be wretched. Remove aversion, then, from all things that are not in our control, and transfer it to things contrary to the nature of what is in our control. But, for the present, totally suppress desire: for, if you desire any of the things which are not in your own control, you must necessarily be disappointed; and of those which are, and which it would be laudable to desire, nothing is yet in your possession. Use only the appropriate actions of pursuit and avoidance; and even these lightly, and with gentleness and reservation.

3

With regard to whatever objects give you delight, are useful, or are deeply loved, remember to tell yourself of what general nature they are, beginning from the most insignificant things. If, for example, you are fond of a specific ceramic cup, remind yourself that it is only ceramic cups in general of which you are fond. Then, if it breaks, you will not be disturbed. If you kiss your child, or your wife, say that you only kiss things which are human, and thus you will not be disturbed if either of them dies.

4

When you are going about any action, remind yourself what nature the action is. If you are going to bathe, picture to yourself the things which usually happen in the bath: some people splash the water, some push, some use abusive language, and others steal. Thus you will more safely go about this action if you say to yourself, "I will now go bathe, and keep my own mind in a state conformable to nature." And in the same manner with regard to every other action. For thus, if any hindrance arises in bathing, you will have it ready to say, "It was not only to bathe that I desired, but to keep my mind in a state conformable to nature; and I will not keep it if I am bothered at things that happen.

5

Men are disturbed, not by things, but by thc principles and notions which they form concerning things. Death, for instance, is not terrible, else it would have appeared so to Socrates. But the terror consists in our notion of death that it is terrible. When therefore we are hindered, or disturbed, or grieved, let us never attribute it to others, but to ourselves; that is, to our own principles. An uninstructed person will lay the fault of his own bad condition upon others. Someone just starting instruction will lay the fault on himself. Some who is perfectly instructed will place blame neither on others nor on himself.

6

Don't be prideful with any excellence that is not your own. If a horse should be prideful and say, "I am handsome," it would be supportable. But when you are prideful, and say, "I have a handsome horse," know that you are proud of what is, in fact, only the good of the horse. What, then, is your own? Only your reaction to the appearances of things. Thus, when you behave conformably to nature in reaction to how things appear, you will be proud with reason; for you will take pride in some good of your own.

7

Consider when, on a voyage, your ship is anchored; if you go on shore to get water you may along the way amuse yourself with picking up a shellfish, or an onion. However, your thoughts and continual attention ought to be bent towards the ship, waiting for the captain to call on board; you must then immediately leave all these things, otherwise you will be thrown into the ship, bound neck and feet like a sheep. So it is with life. If, instead of an onion or a shellfish, you are given a wife or child, that is fine. But if the captain calls, you must run to the ship, leaving them, and regarding none of them. But if you are old, never go far from the ship: lest, when you are called, you should be unable to come in time.

8

Don't demand that things happen as you wish, but wish that they happen as they do happen, and you will go on well.

9

Sickness is a hindrance to the body, but not to your ability to choose, unless that is your choice. Lameness is a hindrance to the leg, but not to your ability to choose. Say this to yourself with regard to everything that happens, then you will see such obstacles as hindrances to something else, but not to yourself.

10

With every accident, ask yourself what abilities you have for making a proper use of it. If you see an attractive person, you will find that self-restraint is the ability you have against your desire. If you are in pain, you will find fortitude. If you hear unpleasant language, you will find patience. And thus habituated, the appearances of things will not hurry you away along with them.

11

Never say of anything, "I have lost it"; but, "I have returned it." Is your child dead? It is returned. Is your wife dead? She is returned. Is your estate taken away? Well, and is not that likewise returned? "But he who took it away is a bad man." What difference is it to you who the giver assigns to take it back? While he gives it to you to possess, take care of it; but don't view it as your own, just as travellers view a hotel.

12

If you want to improve, reject such reasoning's as these: "If I neglect my affairs, I'll have no income; if I don't correct my servant, he will be bad." For it is better to die with hunger, exempt from grief and fear, than to live in affluence with perturbation; and it is better your servant should be bad, than you unhappy.

Begin therefore from little things. Is a little oil spilt? A little wine stolen? Say to yourself, "This is the price paid for equanimity, for tranquillity, and nothing is to be had for nothing." When you call your servant, it is possible that he may not come; or, if he does, he may not do what you want. But he is by no means of such importance that it should be in his power to give you any disturbance.

13

If you want to improve, be content to be thought foolish and stupid with regard to external things. Don't wish to be thought to know anything; and even if you appear to be somebody important to others, distrust yourself. For, it is difficult to both keep your faculty of choice in a state conformable to nature, and at the same time acquire external things. But while you are careful about the one, you must of necessity neglect the other.

14

If you wish your children, and your wife, and your friends to live forever, you are stupid; for you wish to be in control of things which you cannot, you wish for things that belong to others to be your own. So likewise, if you wish your servant to be without fault, you are a fool; for you wish vice not to be vice," but something else. But, if you wish to have your desires undisappointed, this is in your own control. Exercise, therefore, what is in your control. He is the master of every other person who is able to confer or remove whatever that person wishes either to have or to avoid. Whoever, then, would be free, let him wish nothing, let him decline nothing, which depends on others else he must necessarily be a slave.

15

Remember that you must behave in life as at a dinner party. Is anything brought around to you? Put out your hand and take your share with moderation. Does it pass by you? Don't stop it. Is it not yet come? Don't stretch your desire towards it, but wait till it reaches you. Do this with regard to children, to a wife, to public posts, to riches, and you will eventually be a worthy partner of the feasts of the gods. And if you don't even take the things which are set before you, but are able even to reject them, then you will not only be a partner at the feasts of the gods, but also of their empire. For, by doing this, Diogenes, Heraclitus and others like them, deservedly became, and were called, divine.

16

When you see anyone weeping in grief because his son has gone abroad, or is dead, or because he has suffered in his affairs, be careful that the appearance may not misdirect you. Instead, distinguish within your own mind, and be prepared to say, "It's not the accident that distresses this person., because it doesn't distress another person; it is the judgment which he makes about it." As far as words go, however, don't reduce yourself to his level, and certainly do not moan with him. Do not moan inwardly either.

17

Remember that you are an actor in a drama, of such a kind as the author pleases to make it. If short, of a short one; if long, of a long one. If it is his pleasure you should act a poor man, a cripple, a governor, or a private person, see that you act it naturally. For this is your business, to act well the character assigned you; to choose it is another's.

18

When a raven happens to croak unluckily, don't allow the appearance hurry you away with it, but immediately make the distinction to yourself, and say, "None of these things are foretold to me; but either to my paltry body, or property, or reputation, or children, or wife. But to me all omens are lucky, if I will. For whichever of these things happens, it is in my control to derive advantage from it."

19

You may be unconquerable, if you enter into no combat in which it is not in your own control to conquer. When, therefore, you see anyone eminent in honors, or power, or in high esteem on any other account, take heed not to be hurried away with the appearance, and to pronounce him happy; for, if the essence of good consists in things in our own control, there will be no room for envy or emulation. But, for your part, don't wish to be a general, or a senator, or a consul, but to be free; and the only way to this is a contempt of things not in our own control.

20

Remember, that not he who gives ill language or a blow insults, but the principle which represents these things as insulting. When, therefore, anyone provokes you, be assured that it is your own opinion which provokes you. Try, therefore, in the first place, not to be hurried away with the appearance. For if you once gain time and respite, you will more easily command yourself.

21

Let death and exile, and all other things which appear terrible be daily before your eyes, but chiefly death, and you win never entertain any abject thought, nor too eagerly covet anything.

22

If you have an earnest desire of attaining to philosophy, prepare yourself from the very first to be laughed at, to be sneered by the multitude, to hear them say. "He is returned to us a philosopher all at once," and "Whence this supercilious look?" Now, for your part, don't have a supercilious look indeed; but keep steadily to those things which appear best to you as one appointed by God to this station. For remember that, if you adhere to the same point, those very persons who at first ridiculed will afterwards admire you. But if you are conquered by them, you will incur a double ridicule.

23

If you ever happen to turn your attention to externals, so as to wish to please anyone, be assured that you have ruined your scheme of life. Be contented, then, in everything with being a philosopher; and, if you wish to be thought so likewise by anyone, appear so to yourself, and it will suffice you.

24

Don't allow such considerations as these distress you. "I will live in dishonor, and be nobody anywhere." For, if dishonor is an evil, you can no more be involved in any evil by the means of another, than be engaged in anything base. Is it any business of yours, then, to get power, or to be admitted to an entertainment? By no means. How, then, after all, is this a dishonor? And how is it true that you will be nobody anywhere, when you ought to be somebody in those things only which are in your own control, in which you may be of the greatest consequence? "But my friends will be unassisted." – What do you mean by unassisted? They will not have money from you, nor will you make them Roman citizens. Who told you, then, that these are among the things in our own control, and not the affair of others? And who can give to another the things which he has not himself? "Well, but get them, then, that we too may have a share." If I can get them with the preservation of my own honor and fidelity and greatness of mind, show me the way and I will get them; but if you require me to lose my own proper good that you may gain what is not good, consider how inequitable and foolish you are. Besides, which would you rather have, a sum of money, or a friend of fidelity and honor? Rather assist me, then, to gain this character than require me to do those things by which I may lose it. Well, but my country, say you, as far as depends on me, will be unassisted. Here again, what assistance is this you mean? "It will not have porticoes nor baths of your providing." And what signifies that? Why, neither does a smith provide it with shoes, or a shoemaker with arms. It is enough if everyone fully performs his own proper business. And were you to supply it with another citizen of honor and fidelity, would not he be of use to it? Yes. Therefore neither are you yourself useless to it. "What place, then, say you, will I hold in the state?" Whatever you can hold with the preservation of your fidelity and honor. But if, by desiring to be useful to that, you lose these, of what use can you be to your country when you are become faithless and void of shame.

25

Is anyone preferred before you at an entertainment, or in a compliment, or in being admitted to a consultation? If these things are good, you ought to be glad that he has gotten them; and if they are evil, don't be grieved that you have not gotten them. And remember that you cannot, without using the same means [which others do] to acquire things not in our own control, expect to be thought worthy of an equal share of them. For how can he who does not frequent the door of any [great] man, does not attend him, does not praise him, have an equal share with him who does? You are unjust, then, and insatiable, if you are unwilling to pay the price for which these things are sold, and would have them for nothing. For how much is lettuce sold? Fifty cents, for instance. If another, then, paying fifty cents, takes the lettuce, and you, not paying it, go without them, don't imagine that he has gained any advantage over you. For as he has the lettuce, so you have the fifty cents which you did not give. So, in the present case, you have not been invited to such a person's entertainment, because you have not paid him the price for which a supper is sold. It is sold for praise; it is sold for attendance. Give him then the value, if it is for your advantage. But if you would, at the same time, not pay the one and yet receive the other, you are insatiable, and a blockhead. Have you nothing, then, instead of the supper? Yes, indeed, you have: the not praising him, whom you don't like to praise; the not bearing with his behaviour at coming in.

26

The will of nature may be learned from those things in which we don't distinguish from each other. For example, when our neighbor's boy breaks a cup, or the like, we are presently ready to say, "These things will happen." Be assured, then, that when your own cup likewise is broken, you ought to be affected just as when another's cup was broken. Apply this in like manner to greater things. Is the child or wife of another dead? There is no one who would not say, "This is a human accident." but if anyone's own child happens to die, it is presently, "Alas I how wretched am I!" But it should be remembered how we are affected in hearing the same thing concerning others.

27

As a mark is not set up for the sake of missing the aim, so neither does the nature of evil exist in the world.

28

If a person gave your body to any stranger he met on his way, you would certainly be angry. And do you feel no shame in handing over your own mind to be confused and mystified by anyone who happens to verbally attack you?

29

In every affair consider what precedes and follows, and then undertake it. Otherwise you will begin with spirit; but not having thought of the consequences, when some of them appear you will shamefully desist. "I would conquer at the Olympic games." But consider what precedes and follows, and then, if it is for your advantage, engage in the affair. You must conform to rules, submit to a diet, refrain from dainties; exercise your body, whether you choose it or not, at a stated hour, in heat and cold; you must drink no cold water, nor sometimes even wine. In a word, you must give yourself up to your master, as to a physician. Then, in the combat, you may be thrown into a ditch, dislocate your arm, turn your ankle, swallow dust, be whipped, and, after all, lose the victory. When you have evaluated all this, if your inclination still holds, then go to war. Otherwise, take notice, you will behave like children who sometimes play like wrestlers, sometimes gladiators, sometimes blow a trumpet, and sometimes act a tragedy when they have seen and admired these shows. Thus you too will be at one time a wrestler, at another a gladiator, now a philosopher, then an orator; but with your whole soul, nothing at all. Like an ape, you mimic all you see, and one thing after another is sure to please you, but is out of favor as soon as it becomes familiar. For you have never entered upon anything considerately, nor after having viewed the whole matter on all sides, or made any scrutiny into it, but rashly, and with a cold inclination. Thus some, when they have seen a philosopher and heard a man speaking like Euphrates (though, indeed, who can speak like him?), have a mind to be philosophers too. Consider first, man, what the matter is, and what your own nature is able to bear. If you would be a wrestler, consider your shoulders, your back, your thighs; for different persons are made for different things. Do you think that you can act as you do, and be a philosopher? That you can eat and drink, and be angry and discontented as you are now? You must watch, you must labor, you must get the better of certain appetites, must quit your acquaintance, be despised by your servant, be laughed at by those you meet; come off worse than others in everything, in magistracies, in honors, in courts of judicature. When you have considered all these things round, approach, if you please; if, by parting with them, you have a mind to purchase equanimity, freedom, and tranquillity. If not, don't come here; don't, like children, be one while a philosopher, then a publican, then an orator, and then one of Caesar's officers. These things are not consistent. You must be one man, either good or bad. You must cultivate either your own ruling faculty or externals, and apply yourself either to things within or without you; that is, be either a philosopher, or one of the vulgar.

30

Duties are universally measured by relations. Is anyone a father? If so, it is implied that the children should take care of him, submit to him in everything, patiently listen to his reproaches, his correction. But he is a bad father. Is you naturally entitled, then, to a good father? No, only to a father. Is a brother unjust? Well, keep your own situation towards him. Consider not what he does, but what you are to do to keep your own faculty of choice in a state conformable to nature. For another will not hurt you unless you please. You will then be hurt when you think you are hurt. In this manner, therefore, you will find, from the idea of a neighbor, a citizen, a general, the corresponding duties if you accustom yourself to contemplate the several relations.

31

Be assured that the essential property of piety towards the gods is to form right opinions concerning them, as existing “I and as governing the universe with goodness and justice. And fix yourself in this resolution, to obey them, and yield to them, and willingly follow them in all events, as produced by the most perfect understanding. For thus you will never find fault with the gods, nor accuse them as neglecting you. And it is not possible for this to be effected any other way than by withdrawing yourself from things not in our own control, and placing good or evil in those only which are. For if you suppose any of the things not in our own control to be either good or evil, when you are disappointed of what you wish, or incur what you would avoid, you must necessarily find fault with and blame the authors. For every animal is naturally formed to fly and abhor things that appear hurtful, and the causes of them; and to pursue and admire those which appear beneficial, and the causes of them. It is impractical, then, that one who supposes himself to be hurt should be happy about the person who, he thinks, hurts him, just as it is impossible to be happy about the hurt itself. Hence, also, a father is reviled by a son, when he does not impart to him the things which he takes to be good; and the supposing empire to be a good made Polynices and Eteocles mutually enemies. On this account the husbandman, the sailor, the merchant, on this account those who lose wives and children, revile the gods. For where interest is, there too is piety placed. So that, whoever is careful to regulate his desires and aversions as he ought, is, by the very same means, careful of piety likewise. But it is also incumbent on everyone to offer libations and sacrifices and first fruits, conformably to the customs of his country, with purity, and not in a slovenly manner, nor negligently, nor sparingly, nor beyond his ability.

32

When you have recourse to divination, remember that you know not what the event will be, and you come to learn it of the diviner; but of what nature it is you know before you come, at least if you are a philosopher. For if it is among the things not in our own control, it can by no means be either good or evil. Don't, therefore, bring either desire or aversion with you to the diviner (else you will approach him trembling), but first acquire a distinct knowledge that every event is indifferent and nothing to you., of whatever sort it may be, for it will be in your power to make a right use of it, and this no one can hinder; then come with confidence to the gods, as your counselors, and afterwards, when any counsel is given you, remember what counselors you have assumed, and whose advice you will neglect if you disobey. Come to divination, as Socrates prescribed, in cases of which the whole consideration relates to the event, and in which no opportunities are afforded by reason, or any other art, to discover the thing proposed to be learned. When, therefore, it is our duty to share the danger of a friend or of our country, we ought not to consult the oracle whether we will share it with them or not. For, though the diviner should forewarn you that the victims are unfavourable, this means no more than that either death or mutilation or exile is portended. But we have reason within us, and it directs, even with these hazards, to the greater diviner, the Pythian god, who cast out of the temple the person who gave no assistance to his friend while another was murdering him.

33

Immediately prescribe some character and form of conduce to yourself, which you may keep both alone and in company.

Be for the most part silent, or speak merely what is necessary, and in few words. We may, however, enter, though sparingly, into discourse sometimes when occasion calls for it, but not on any of the common subjects, of gladiators, or horse races, or athletic champions, or feasts, the vulgar topics of conversation; but principally not of men, so as either to blame, or praise, or make comparisons. If you are able, then, by your own conversation bring over that of your company to proper subjects; but, if you happen to be taken among strangers, be silent.

Don't allow your laughter be much, nor on many occasions, nor profuse.

Avoid swearing, if possible, altogether; if not, as far as you are able.

Avoid public and vulgar entertainments; but, if ever an occasion calls you to them, keep your attention upon the stretch, that you may not imperceptibly slide into vulgar manners. For be assured that if a person be ever so sound himself, yet, if his companion be infected, he who converses with him will be infected likewise.

Provide things relating to the body no further than mere use; as meat, drink, clothing, house, family. But strike off and reject everything relating to show and delicacy.

As far as possible, before marriage, keep yourself pure from familiarities with women, and, if you indulge them, let it be lawfully." But don't therefore be troublesome and full of reproofs to those who use these liberties, nor frequently boast that you yourself don't.

If anyone tells you that such a person speaks ill of you, don't make excuses about what is said of you, but answer: "He does not know my other faults, else he would not have mentioned only these."

It is not necessary for you to appear often at public spectacles; but if ever there is a proper occasion for you to be there, don't appear more solicitous for anyone than for yourself; that is, wish things to be only just as they are, and him only to conquer who is the conqueror, for thus you will meet with no hindrance. But abstain entirely from declamations and derision and violent emotions. And when you come away, don't discourse a great deal on what has passed, and what does not contribute to your own amendment. For it would appear by such discourse that you were immoderately struck with the show.

Go not [of your own accord] to the rehearsals of any *authors*, nor appear [at them] readily. But, if you do appear, keep your gravity and sedateness, and at the same time avoid being morose.

When you are going to confer with anyone, and particularly of those in a superior station, represent to yourself how Socrates or Zeno would behave in such a case, and you will not be at a loss to make a proper use of whatever may occur.

When you are going to any of the people in power, represent to yourself that you will not find him at home; that you will not be admitted; that the doors will not be opened to you; that he will take no notice of you. If, with all this, it is your duty to go, bear what happens, and never say [to yourself], "It was not worth so much." For this is vulgar, and like a man dazed by external things.

In parties of conversation, avoid a frequent and excessive mention of your own actions and dangers.

For, however agreeable it may be to yourself to mention the risks you have run, it is not equally agreeable to others to hear your adventures. Avoid, likewise, an endeavour to excite laughter. For this is a slippery point, which may throw you into vulgar manners, and, besides, may be apt to lessen you in the esteem of your acquaintance. Approaches to indecent discourse are likewise dangerous. Whenever, therefore, anything of this sort happens, if there be a proper opportunity, rebuke him who makes advances that way; or, at least, by silence and blushing and a forbidding look, show yourself to be displeased by such talk.

34

If you are struck by the appearance of any promised pleasure, guard yourself against being hurried away by it; but let the affair wait your leisure, and procure yourself some delay. Then bring to your mind both points of time: that in which you will enjoy the pleasure, and that in which you will repent and reproach yourself after you have enjoyed it; and set before you, in opposition to these, how you will be glad and applaud yourself if you abstain. And even though it should appear to you a seasonable gratification, take heed that its enticing, and agreeable and attractive force may not subdue you; but set in opposition to this how much better it is to be conscious of having gained so great a victory.

35

When you do anything from a clear judgment that it ought to be done, never shun the being seen to do it, even though the world should make a wrong supposition about it; for, if you don't act right, shun the action itself; but, if you do, why are you afraid of those who censure you wrongly?

36

As the proposition, "Either it is day or it is night," is extremely proper for a disjunctive argument, but quite improper in a conjunctive one, so, at a feast, to choose the largest share is very suitable to the bodily appetite, but utterly inconsistent with the social spirit of an entertainment. When you eat with another, then, remember not only the value of those things which are set before you to the body, but the value of that behaviour which ought to be observed towards the person who gives the entertainment.

37

If you have assumed any character above your strength, you have both made an ill figure in that and quitted one which you might have supported.

38

When walking, you are careful not to step on a nail or turn your foot; so likewise be careful not to hurt the ruling faculty of your mind. And, if we were to guard against this in every action, we should undertake the action with the greater safety.

39

The body is to everyone the measure of the possessions proper for it, just as the foot is of the shoe. If, therefore, you stop at this, you will keep the measure; but if you move beyond it, you must necessarily be carried forward, as down a cliff; as in the case of a shoe, if you go beyond its fitness to the foot, it comes first to be gilded, then purple, and then studded with jewels. For to that which once exceeds a due measure, there is no bound.

40

Women from fourteen years old are flattered with the title of "mistresses" by the men. Therefore, perceiving that they are regarded only as qualified to give the men pleasure, they begin to adorn themselves, and in that to place ill their hopes. We should, therefore, fix our attention on making them sensible that they are valued for the appearance of decent, modest and discreet behavior.

41

It is a mark of want of genius to spend much time in things relating to the body, as to be long in our exercises, in eating and drinking, and in the discharge of other animal functions. These should be done incidentally and slightly, and our whole attention be engaged in the care of the understanding.

42

When any person harms you, or speaks badly of you, remember that he acts or speaks from a supposition of its being his duty. Now, it is not possible that he should follow what appears right to you, but what appears so to himself. Therefore, if he judges from a wrong appearance, he is the person hurt, since he too is the person deceived. For if anyone should suppose a true proposition to be false, the proposition is not hurt, but he who is deceived about it. Setting out, then, from these principles, you will meekly bear a person who reviles you, for you will say upon every occasion, "It seemed so to him."

43

Everything has two handles, the one by which it may be carried, the other by which it cannot. If your brother acts unjustly, don't lay hold on the action by the handle of his injustice, for by that it cannot be carried; but by the opposite, that he is your brother, that he was brought up with you; and thus you will lay hold on it, as it is to be carried.

44

These reasoning's are unconnected: "I am richer than you, therefore I am better"; "I am more eloquent than you, therefore I am better." The connection is rather this: "I am richer than you, therefore my property is greater than yours;" "I am more eloquent than you, therefore my style is better than yours." But you, after all, are neither property nor style.

45

Does anyone bathe in a mighty little time? Don't say that he does it ill, but in a mighty little time. Does anyone drink a great quantity of wine? Don't say that he does ill, but that he drinks a great quantity. For, unless you perfectly understand the principle from which anyone acts, how should you know if he acts ill? Thus you will not run the hazard of assenting to any appearances but such as you fully comprehend.

46

Never call yourself a philosopher, nor talk a great deal among the unlearned about theorems, but act conformably to them. Thus, at an entertainment, don't talk how persons ought to eat, but eat as you ought. For remember that in this manner Socrates also universally avoided all ostentation. And when persons came to him and desired to be recommended by him to philosophers, he took and- recommended them, so well did he bear being overlooked. So that if ever any talk should happen among the unlearned concerning philosophic theorems, be you, for the most part, silent. For there is great danger in immediately throwing out what you have not digested. And, if anyone tells you that you know nothing, and you are not nettled at it, then you may be sure that you have begun your business. For sheep don't throw up the grass to show the shepherds how much they have eaten; but, inwardly digesting their food, they outwardly produce wool and milk. Thus, therefore, do you likewise not show theorems to the unlearned, but the actions produced by them after they have been digested.

47

When you have brought yourself to supply the necessities of your body at a small price, don't pique yourself upon it; nor, if you drink water, be saying upon every occasion, "I drink water." But first consider how much more sparing and patient of hardship the poor are than we. But if at any time you would inure yourself by exercise to labor, and bearing hard trials, do it for your own sake, and not for the world; don't grasp statues, but, when you are violently thirsty, take a little cold water in your mouth, and spurt it out and tell nobody.

48

The condition and characteristic of a vulgar person, is, that he never expects either benefit or hurt from himself, but from externals. The condition and characteristic of a philosopher is, that he expects all hurt and benefit from himself. The marks of a proficient are, that he censures no one, praises no one, blames no one, accuses no one, says nothing concerning himself as being anybody, or knowing anything: when he is, in any instance, hindered or restrained, he accuses himself; and, if he is praised, he secretly laughs at the person who praises him; and, if he is censured, he makes no defence. But he goes about with the caution of sick or injured people, dreading to move anything that is set right, before it is perfectly fixed. He suppresses all desire in himself; he transfers his aversion to those things only which thwart the proper use of our own faculty of choice; the exertion of his active powers towards anything is very gentle; if he appears stupid or ignorant, he does not care, and, in a word, he watches himself as an enemy, and one in ambush.

49

When anyone shows himself overly confident in ability to understand and interpret the works of Chrysippus, say to yourself, "Unless Chrysippus had written obscurely, this person would have had no subject for his vanity. But what do I desire? To understand nature and follow her. I ask, then, who interprets her, and, finding Chrysippus does, I have recourse to him. I don't understand his writings. I seek, therefore, one to interpret them." So far there is nothing to value myself upon. And when I find an interpreter, what remains is to make use of his instructions. This alone is the valuable thing. But, if I admire nothing but merely the interpretation, what do I become more than a grammarian instead of a philosopher? Except, indeed, that instead of Homer I interpret Chrysippus. When anyone, therefore, desires me to read Chrysippus to him, I rather blush when I cannot show my actions agreeable and consonant to his discourse.

50

Whatever moral rules you have deliberately proposed to yourself. abide by them as they were laws, and as if you would be guilty of impiety by violating any of them. Don't regard what anyone says of you, for this, after all, is no concern of yours. How long, then, will you put off thinking yourself worthy of the highest improvements and follow the distinctions of reason? You have received the philosophical theorems, with which you ought to be familiar, and you have been familiar with them. What other master, then, do you wait for, to throw upon that the delay of reforming yourself? You are no longer a boy, but a grown man. If, therefore, you will be negligent and slothful, and always add procrastination to procrastination, purpose to purpose, and fix day after day in which you will attend to yourself, you will insensibly continue without proficiency, and, living and dying, persevere in being one of the vulgar. This instant, then, think yourself worthy of living as a man grown up, and a proficient. Let whatever appears to be the best bet to you an inviolable law. And if any instance of pain or pleasure, or glory or disgrace, is set before you, remember that now is the combat, now the Olympiad comes on, nor can it be put off. By once being defeated and giving way, proficiency is lost, or by the contrary preserved. Thus Socrates became perfect, improving himself by everything. attending to nothing but reason. And though you are not yet a Socrates, you ought, however, to live as one desirous of becoming a Socrates.

51

The first and most necessary topic in philosophy is that of the use of moral theorems, such as, “We ought not to lie;” the second is that of demonstrations, such as, “What is the origin of our obligation not to lie;” the third gives strength and articulation to the other two, such as, “What is the origin of this is a demonstration.” For what is demonstration? What is consequence? What contradiction? What truth? What falsehood? The third topic, then, is necessary on the account of the second, and the second on the account of the first. But the most necessary, and that whereon we ought to rest, is the first. But we act just on the contrary. For we spend all our time on the third topic, and employ all our diligence about that, and entirely neglect the first. Therefore, at the same time that we lie, we are immediately prepared to show how it is demonstrated that lying is not right.

52

Upon all occasions we ought to have these maxims ready at hand:

"Conduct me, Jove, and you, oh Destiny,
Wherever your decrees have fixed my station."
Cleanthes

"I follow cheerfully; and, did I not,
Wicked and wretched, I must follow still
Whoever yields properly to Fate, is deemed
Wise among men, and knows the laws of heaven."
Euripides, Frag. 965

And this third:

"O Crito, if it thus pleases the gods, thus let it be. Anytus and Melitus may kill me indeed, but hurt me they cannot."

Plato's Crito and Apology

INTERNATIONAL BESTSELLER

THE POWER OF YOUR SUBCONSCIOUS MIND

by Dr. Joseph Murphy

Pages : 232
Size : 8 x 5.25 inches
Binding : Paperback
Language : English
Subject : Self-Help
ISBN : 9788180320958

'The Power of Your Subconscious Mind' has been a bestseller since its first publication in 1963, selling many millions of copies since its original publication. It is one of the most brilliant and beloved spiritual self-help works of all time which can help you heal yourself, banish your fears, sleep better, enjoy better relationships and just feel happier. The techniques are simple and results come quickly. You can improve your relationships, your finances, your physical well-being.

Dr Joseph Murphy explains that life events are actually the result of the workings of your conscious and subconscious minds. He suggests practical techniques through which one can change one's destiny, principally by focusing and redirecting this miraculous energy. Years of research studying the world's major religions convinced him that some Great Power lay behind all spiritual life and that this power is within each of us.

'The Power of Your Subconscious Mind' will open a world of success, happiness, prosperity, and peace for you.

OTHER BOOKS YOU MAY LIKE

- 1984 by George Orwell, ISBN: 9789380914947
- 12 Years a Slave by Solomon Northup, ISBN: 9789390492374
- 51 Most Powerful Prayers by Ryan, ISBN: 9789354990847
- A Christmas Carol by Charles Dickens, ISBN: 9788193545874
- A Cloud by Day, a Fire by Night by AW Tozer, ISBN: 9789354990854
- A Passage to India by E.M. Forster, ISBN: 9789354990205
- A Room of One's Own by Virginia Woolf, ISBN: 9789354990281
- A Streetcar Named Desire by Tennessee Williams, ISBN: 9788194748601
- A Wrinkle in Time by Madeleine L'Engle, ISBN: 9789354991066
- Abraham Lincoln by Lord Charnwood, ISBN: 9789380914251
- Absolute Surrender by Andrew Murray, ISBN: 9789389716269
- Animal Farm by George Orwell, ISBN: 9789380914701
- Anthem by Ayn Rand, ISBN: 9789389157079
- As a Man Thinketh by James Allen, ISBN: 9788180320262
- As I Lay Dying by William Faulkner, ISBN: 9789390492381
- Awakened Imagination by Neville Goddard, ISBN: 9789389157086
- Be What You Wish by Neville Goddard, ISBN: 9789387669550
- Chanakya Neeti by Chanakya, ISBN: 9789389716276
- Civilization and Its Discontents by Sigmund Freud, ISBN: 9789387669499
- Delighting in God by AW Tozer, ISBN: 9788194748632
- Demian by Hermann Hesse, ISBN: 9789387669567
- Experiencing the Holy Spirit by Andrew Murray, ISBN: 9788194764809
- Feeling is the Secret by Neville Goddard, ISBN: 9789389157109
- George Orwell Combo : Animal Farm & 1984, ISBN: 9789390492459
- Gravity by George Gamow, ISBN: 9789388118484
- Guerrilla Warfare by Ernesto Che Guevara, ISBN: 9789354990366

Develop your reading habit | **Gift books to your friends**

OTHER BOOKS YOU MAY LIKE

- How to be filled with the Holy Spirit by AW Tozer, ISBN: 9789389157116
- How to Develop Self Confidence by Dale Carnegie, ISBN: 9789387669000
- In His Steps by Charles M. Sheldon, ISBN: 9789390492794
- Life of Christ by Fulton J. Sheen, ISBN: 9789389716306
- Lost Horizon by James Hilton, ISBN: 9789389716313
- Man: The Dwelling Place of God by AW Tozer, ISBN: 9789354990656
- Maneaters of Kumaon by Jim Corbett, ISBN: 9789354990731
- Mansarover 1 (Hindi) by Premchand, ISBN: 9789380914978
- Mansarover 2 (Hindi) by Premchand, ISBN: 9789380914985
- Meditation and Its Methods by Swami Vivekananda, ISBN: 9789389716320
- One, None and a Hundred Thousand by Luigi Pirandello, ISBN: 9789389716337
- Paths to Power by AW Tozer, ISBN: Forthcoming
- Scientific Healing Affirmations by P. Yogananda, ISBN: 9789389716344
- Selected Stories of Rabindranath Tagore by Tagore, ISBN: 9789380914770
- Siddhartha by Hermann Hesse, ISBN: 9789380914145
- Student's Encyclopedia of G. K. by GP Editors, ISBN: 9789380914190
- Tales from Shakespeare by Charles Lamb & Mary Lamb, ISBN: 9789380914367
- The Alchemy of Happiness by Al-Ghazzali, ISBN: 9789387669505
- The Book of Enoch by Enoch, ISBN: 9789390492480
- The Dynamic Laws of Prosperity by Catherine Ponder, ISBN: 9789388118156
- The Game of Life and How to Play It by Florence Shinn, ISBN: 9789387669390
- The Imitation of Christ by Thomas À Kempis, ISBN: 9789388118057
- The Knowledge of the Holy by AW Tozer, ISBN: 9789389157130
- The Law by Neville Goddard, ISBN: 9789390492886
- The Light of Asia by Sir Edwin Arnold, ISBN: 9789380914923
- The Magic of Believing by Claudie Bristol, ISBN: 9789388118149

Develop your reading habit | **Gift books to your friends**

OTHER BOOKS YOU MAY LIKE

- The Magic of Faith by Joseph Murphy, ISBN: 9789388118743
- The Miracles of Your Mind by Joseph Murphy, ISBN: 9788180320743
- The Mysterious Affair at Styles by Agatha Christie, ISBN: 9789390492510
- The Origin of Species by Charles Darwin, ISBN: 9788180320453
- The Plague by Albert Camus, ISBN: 9788194764892
- The Power of Awareness by Neville Goddard, ISBN: 9789387669406
- The Power of Positive Thinking by Norman Vincent Peale, ISBN: 9789388118569
- The Problem of Increasing Human Energy by Nikola Tesla, ISBN: 9789354990953
- The Prophet by Kahlil Gibran, ISBN: 9789380914022
- The Psychopathology of Everyday Life by Sigmund Freud, ISBN: 9789388118071
- The Pursuit of God by AW Tozer, ISBN: 9789389157147
- The Railway Children by E Nesbit, ISBN: 9789354990960
- The Red Badge of Courage by Stephen Crane, ISBN: 9789354990977
- The Sound and the Fury by William Faulkner, ISBN: 9789390492572
- The Stranger by Albert Camus, ISBN: 9789390492589
- The Sun Also Rises by Ernest Hemingway, ISBN: 9789354990984
- The Yoga Sutras of Patanjali by Patanjali, ISBN: 9789389716351
- Their Eyes Were Watching God by Zora Neale Hurston, ISBN: 9788194764885
- Think and Grow Rich by Napoleon Hill, ISBN: 9788180320255
- Thought Vibration by William Walker Atkinson, ISBN: 9789389157154
- To the Lighthouse by Virginia Woolf, ISBN: 9789390492190
- Who were the Shudras by Dr B.R. Ambedkar, ISBN: 9789354991028
- World's Best Short Stories: Volume 1 by Various Authors, ISBN: 9789390492275
- Wuthering Heights by Emily Brontë, ISBN: 9788193545898
- Your Faith is Your Fortune by Neville Goddard, ISBN: 9789389157161
- Zen in the Art of Archery by Eugen Herrigel, ISBN: 9789354991059

Develop your reading habit | **Gift books to your friends**

www.ingramcontent.com/pod-product-compliance
Ingram Content Group UK Ltd.
Pitfield, Milton Keynes, MK11 3LW, UK
UKHW032043260826
14628UKWH00008B/3133

9 789354 993817

BESTSELLING CHRISTIAN BOOKS

- 51 Most Powerful Prayers by Ryan
  Christianity/Prayers, ISBN: 9789354990847
- A Christmas Carol by Charles Dickens
  Christianity, ISBN: 9788193545874
- A Cloud by Day, a Fire by Night by AW Tozer
  Christianity/Inspiration, ISBN: 9789354990854
- Absolute Surrender by Andrew Murray
  Christianity, ISBN: 9789389716269
- Awakened Imagination by Neville Goddard
  Christianity, ISBN: 9789389157086
- Be What You Wish by Neville Goddard
  Christianity, ISBN: 9789387669550
- Delighting in God by AW Tozer
  Christianity/Good & Evil, ISBN: 9788194748632
- Experiencing the Holy Spirit by Andrew Murray
  Christianity, ISBN: 9788194764809
- Feeling is the Secret by Neville Goddard
  Christianity, ISBN: 9789389157109
- How to be Filled with the Holy Spirit by AW Tozer
  Christianity, ISBN: 9789389157116
- In His Steps by Charles M. Sheldon
  Christianity, ISBN: 9789390492794
- Life of Christ by Fulton J. Sheen
  Christianity/New Testament, ISBN: 9789389716306

Search the book by its ISBN

BESTSELLING CHRISTIAN BOOKS

- Man: The Dwelling Place of God by AW Tozer
  Christianity, ISBN: 9789354990656
- Paths to Power by AW Tozer
  Christianity/Discipleship, ISBN: Forthcoming
- The Alchemy of Happiness by Al-Ghazzali
  Christianity, ISBN: 9789387669505
- The Imitation of Christ by Thomas À Kempis
  Christianity, ISBN: 9789388118057
- The Knowledge of the Holy by AW Tozer
  Christianity/Sermons, ISBN: 9789389157130
- The Law by Neville Goddard
  Christianity, ISBN: 9789390492886
- The Magic of Believing by Claudie Bristol
  Christianity, ISBN: 9789388118149
- The Magic of Faith by Joseph Murphy
  Christianity, ISBN: 9789388118743
- The Miracles of Your Mind by Joseph Murphy
  Christianity, ISBN: 9788180320743
- The Power of Awareness by Neville Goddard
  Christianity, ISBN: 9789387669406
- The Pursuit of God by AW Tozer
  Christianity, ISBN: 9789389157147
- Your Faith is Your Fortune by Neville Goddard
  Christianity, ISBN: 9789389157161

Search the book by its ISBN